DEAN RUSK

THE AMERICAN REVOLUTION AND THE FUTURE

Distinguished Lecture Series
on
the Bicentennial

This lecture is one in a series sponsored
by the American Enterprise Institute
in celebration of the Bicentennial of the United States.
The views expressed are those of the lecturers
and do not necessarily reflect
the views of the staff, officers or trustees of AEI.
All of the lectures in this series will be
collected later in a single volume.

revolution · continuity · promise

DEAN RUSK

THE AMERICAN REVOLUTION AND THE FUTURE

Delivered in
Ford's Theatre, Washington, D. C.
on June 17, 1974

American Enterprise Institute for Public Policy Research
Washington, D. C.

ISBN 0-8447-1316-3

Library of Congress Catalog Card Number L.C. 75-865

Printed in the United States of America

I am greatly complimented by the opportunity to come here to Ford's Theatre, a place hallowed by the life and death of one of our greatest Americans, to talk about the American Revolution and its meaning for the future. In preparing these remarks, my first reaction was to wonder whether this is the time to address such matters, whether the present sense of dismay and concern would make words about first principles sound hollow, whether cynicism might take over, whether it might be better to wait. But further reflection suggested that it is in just such a time that we need to remind ourselves of some rather elementary guidelines to lead us through the fog of confusion and to help reestablish our sense of direction.

For example: where are the voices that are saying to the American people that 99-plus percent of the men and women in government—executive, legislative and judicial branches, federal, state and local—are honest, decent men and women trying to do a good job? Are we by silence or by innuendo allowing tens of millions of the members of a major political party in this country to bear the malefactions of some three dozen people, however highly placed some of them might have been? Our incumbents, whatever their party, are feeling the backlash of recent events without regard to their own guilt or innocence. Surely there are certain elements of fairness and justice which we can draw upon to check some of the extravagancies of our period, whatever our dismay might be at some of the things which have happened.

What can I say about the future? Anyone who attempts to talk about the future must be respectful of the pervasive fog which hides much of it from our view. Those who are accustomed to the fact that most foreign policy decisions are about the future will know that there is no way to describe in detail what life will be like in the year 2000. Indeed, life in the American colonies was much nearer the life of the Greek city-states than that of twentieth century America. And historic literature is filled with prophesies gone wrong. For example, it was once believed that if trains moved at more than forty miles an hour, the blood vessels of all persons on board would burst because the human body could not stand such speed. And some held that the introduction of bathtubs would bring pestilence upon the land.

It is possible, however, to identify some major issues which must preoccupy us between now and the year 2000, some different in kind from any the human race has ever before faced and some likely to impose the severest strains upon all existing political systems as necessary adjustments are made. Some will require a relatively definitive solution rather soon if the human race is to survive. Nostalgia for simpler and more leisurely days offers us no escape from the continuing and breathtaking acceleration in the pace of change, no relief from the ever growing complexity of individual, national and international life.

A very wise man, General Omar Bradley, said a number of years ago that the time had come to chart our course by the distant stars and not by the lights of each passing ship. Which are the ideas that can give us our compass bearings amidst the tumult of change? We would do no honor to Thomas Jefferson and his extraordinary colleagues of the Continental Congress were we to celebrate our bicentennial by ritual incantation of a few words, with bands playing and flags flying. What do those ideas mean today? Where are the universal men and the universal women, people like Benjamin Franklin and Thomas Jefferson, to help us see things as a whole and derive from the masses of specialized knowledge those insights and flashes of wisdom so vital to the dignity and freedom of man? One can retain a profound respect for the value of scholarly research in the traditional sense and still hope that our universities would do somewhat more to find a way to discover and nourish more Jeffersons, more Tocquevilles, more Lord Bryces.

2

I

Let us pause at this point to remind ourselves of a few of the problems which will be with us for the decades just ahead. Our overriding concern must be the organization of a durable peace. The fact that men have fought each other since the dawn of human history leads many to suppose that war among nations is inevitable—rooted in the very nature of man. But most of us in this room have been witnesses to a profound change in the nature of the problem: the appearance in frail human hands of thousands of megatons of nuclear weaponry that could, if fired, bring into question the capacity of our fragile earth to sustain human life. My generation was led into the catastrophe of a world war which could have been prevented. We came out of it with a deep commitment to the notion of collective security, a commitment written into Article I of the United Nations Charter and later reinforced by mutual security treaties. We must be honest and recognize that acceptance of the concept of collective security is steadily eroding. One can understand why that should be so in this country: it has cost us dearly in the form of the lives of thousands of our young men and very large economic burdens to try to sustain a little peace here and there in different parts of the world. For Americans, collective security has not been all that collective: we put up 90 percent of the non-Korean forces in Korea and 80 percent of the non-Vietnamese forces in Vietnam.

I can understand those who say, "If this is what collective security means, maybe it is not a very good idea." I am concerned, however, that there is not enough public discussion on how to organize a durable peace, if not through collective security. To this question, each generation must find its own answer. I myself do not attempt to advise today's young people on how to answer the question. They must find out for themselves. Their answer may not be as simplistic as collective security; it may be far more complicated, like a bundle of sticks, no one of which is enough to do the job, but which all together might get it accomplished. I have suggested to some of my young friends that they would not improve their situation very much if they merely rejected the

mistakes of their fathers in order to embrace the mistakes of their grandfathers.

Our young people have some important assets on which to build. In two months time we shall be passing through the twenty-ninth year since a nuclear weapon has been fired in anger, a very important statement to be able to make when one looks back upon the grievous crises through which we have come since 1945. One can also say with complete accuracy that the overwhelming majority of international frontiers are peaceful, the overwhelming majority of treaties are complied with, and the overwhelming majority of disputes are settled by peaceful means. If that is not your impression, it is partly because there is a vast context of habitual and regular international cooperation which fails to come to your attention, not because it is secret, but because it cannot compete with the troubles of our age for the limited space and time at the disposal of our news media.

The search for peace must continue, probing every possibility for agreement before problems rise to the point of violence. Emphasis must be upon prevention—upon reducing problems one at a time, large or small, to manageable dimensions.

Consider the environment. We have learned in recent years that man can inflict irreparable damage upon the thin skin around the surface of the earth which we call the biosphere, a few inches of top soil, a little water, and about two miles of atmosphere above which most humans need assistance. On this issue I am relatively optimistic, because I believe we have a chance to take it up while it is merely serious—before it becomes disastrous. There is growing international concern about the environment and increasing national and local action, particularly among the industrialized nations. We are familiar with the general notion *sic utere tuo,* that one should use one's own in such a way as not to damage one's neighbor. Such cases as *Georgia v. Tennessee Copper Company,* the Trails Smelter arbitration, and the Corfu Channel case before the International Court of Justice pointed the way toward international responsibility for environmental damage. My guess is that we shall come to the concept of trust, a trust relationship to the air and water which are with us but briefly before moving on for the use of others. The biosphere is literally a common heritage

4

of mankind, for which we all have a responsibility. I hope we live up to our obligations.

One, of course, must point to the population explosion as a major item on our agenda for the future. Even if the industrialized countries reach a relatively stable population by the year 2000, which is possible, and if the developing countries do the same by the year 2030, which is somewhat less likely, the population of the world will level off sometime within a century at 13.5 billion. This has enormous implications for food, housing, jobs, raw materials, the amenities of life, education, and medical care. It is interesting to note that since 1945 no nation, regardless of its ideology, has been basing a policy of territorial expansion upon what Hitler called Lebensraum—living space. We have all been relying upon science and technology to somehow take care of our minimum needs. Somewhere along the way that hope will evaporate, and once again burgeoning populations could become a cause of war, as they have since the dawn of human history. I see little comfort in the Malthusian truism that if population outruns foodstuffs, then starvation, war or pestilence will bring the population back into balance. Such answers are not acceptable to most human beings, and we shall have to undertake the most rigorous efforts to find other answers, answers tolerable to the conscience of man. This year, 1974, is United Nations Population Year and we are very fortunate indeed to have a great Mexican statesman, Antonio Carillo Flores, as the head of that effort. At the present stage of human history, we are still free to approach the problem of population control on a voluntary basis, but not far down the road our successors may have to face the agonizing problem of applying the restraints of law, both national and international.

Our agenda must include relations among races, religions, and cultural traditions. It has been only by the skin of our teeth that we have avoided in this postwar period, as the great colonial empires have disappeared, a confrontation between the white race and the rest of the world's peoples. Wherever around the world there are different races or different religions, cultures, and nationality traditions, there are problems. What is happening here in the United States is of the greatest importance and is being watched most intently by many in other lands—not just because they want to know whether we shall succeed in our determination to find better answers than we have found before, but because if we can succeed, they can draw upon that experience for ideas which might be highly relevant to their own problems.

And then there are the prospective shortages of raw materials and energy sources. We all know by now that 6 percent of the world's population—the people of the United States—consumes almost 50 percent of the world's raw materials and energy. When we think of all the imported materials vital to our current way of life—chromium, platinum, cobalt, tin, manganese, nickel, bauxite, mercury, tungsten, zinc, iron ore and, above all, oil—we realize that we are not as rich as we thought. A little more than a year ago, a Soviet representative to a United Nations body said that the earth can support only one United States, implying that if the other nations of the world should come anywhere near our productivity and our rates of consumption, the old earth itself would just groan and collapse.

Clearly, something is going to have to give. I was very pleased that this past week the Senate approved a National Commission on Supplies and Shortages. There is a possibility that this commission will recommend that a more permanent body be set up to give intensive study to the long-range aspects of these matters— a body which would keep up-to-date the important work of the Paley Commission of the Truman administration and widely disseminate its findings so that all citizens can know the situation and decide what to do. My guess is that we shall face over the next decade a reduction in the consumption of material things and that we shall be seeking more satisfaction from services and the pursuits of leisure.

Also of concern for the future are the implications of rapidly developing science and technology. I have been somewhat encouraged by the increasing discourse between scientists and their colleagues in the social sciences and the humanities and by the increased attention in the departments of government to the problems growing out of the work in our laboratories. We are beginning to confront what to me are extraordinarily difficult questions for which I do not pretend to have answers. Are we nearing the point when society must give some direction to our scientists about the Pandora's boxes on which they are working? In fact, we already are trying this in the field of biological warfare. What about

6

weather modification? It is one thing to turn hail into rain or to remove fog from an airport, but would be quite another matter if we should develop the capacity to bring about large-scale changes in world weather and climatic patterns. Finally—and perhaps this is a sign that your speaker is old-fashioned—what about certain types of laboratory experimentation in human genetics that raise the possibility of alteration in the structure and nature of man? Think hard on that one.

We must also think about the future in terms of social justice. Here, perhaps, I have a bias; if so, you may at least understand it. I happen to believe that for the next decade or two the agenda for our needs within this country can largely be found in the extraordinary legislative program enacted by the Congress during the presidency of Lyndon Johnson. Of course elements of the program must be tested and refined—more limited here, more effective financing there. Improvements are needed because Lyndon Johnson was a man in a very great hurry. Nevertheless, his concerns are now a part of our national agenda, and if we postpone them today we shall simply have to face them tomorrow when they might be even more difficult to resolve.

Abroad there is also a notion of social justice, which has to do with just as vital a matter as war and peace: the serious gap between the have and the have-not nations. It is easy to be weary of the burden of foreign aid. But consider the consequences if we should try to develop a trillion dollar gross national product here in the United States in the midst of a world pressed with grinding poverty, pestilence, and violence.

What do these problems have to do with Thomas Jefferson, with the Continental Congress, and the Declaration of Independence? They came before railways, ocean liners, automobiles, airplanes, radio, television, $E = MC^2$, and men driving "jeeps" around the moon. But the men of the Continental Congress were heirs to more than two thousand years of discourse on the political consequences of the nature of man. We are indebted to my friend, the late Clinton Rossiter, who described this heritage brilliantly in his *Seed Time of the Republic,* a book which should be widely read and reread during the bicentennial season. Thomas Jefferson did not claim that he and his fellows created the ideas we find in the Declaration. What he did do was articulate in eloquent simplicity, in little more than two hundred words, ideas which represented a broad consensus of the men of his time and which were well-suited to the purposes which they had in mind.

These ideas were rooted in the work and thought of Herodotus, Thucydides, Plutarch, Cicero, Tacitus, Vattell, Pufendorf, Grotius, Locke, Montesquieu, Burke, and great common lawyers such as Coke and Blackstone. They also grew out of the experience of the Greek city-states, the majesty of Roman law, the Judaeo-Christian ethic, the emphasis of the Protestant Revolution upon the individual, the great debate about natural law, the restraints upon raw power achieved from the writing of the Magna Carta through the English Revolution of 1688, and the emerging gaps between the rights of Englishmen in England and the rights of Englishmen across the seas in the American colonies.

There is one idea articulated in the Declaration which seems to me to be a permanent part of our intellectual and political equipment—the simple principle that governments derive their just powers from the consent of the governed. Philosophers and historians have been somewhat critical of this principle because it seemed somehow to be rooted in the social contract idea posited by such men as Locke, Hobbes and Rousseau. I suppose we could agree with the historians that we can find no single moment when such a contract came into being—although I suggest that the years from 1776 through 1789 came as close to witnessing the development of a social contract as is likely to be seen in the real world. But the social contract was a figure of speech, even for those who wrote about it. It was a tool of analysis, and perhaps a rather useful one. Its strength may well derive from the inadequacy of the alternatives. If not consent of the governed, what? Feudal fealty? Divine right? Class dictatorship? Rule by an elite, whether philosopher-kings or technocrats? If government is not rooted in the people, where then?

My own view is that the notion that governments derive their just powers from the consent of the governed remains the most powerful and revolutionary political idea of the world today. Tyrants live in terror of this simple idea and sometimes take the most extraordinary measures to ensure that their people are not infected by this virus of freedom.

This does not mean that we were committed by the Continental Congress to embark upon a crusade to remake other political systems in our own image. There should be the greatest diversity in political organization, including the means by which the popular will can be registered or taken into account.

The idea of popular sovereignty has served as a scarlet thread of American policy over the years. This is why our closest friends are constitutional or parliamentary democracies. This is the source of our concern about some of the things which have gone on under totalitarian regimes. This is why we have welcomed into the world community more than seventy new independent nations. This is why we are so deeply concerned about our own failures here at home in living up to the great promises of our Declaration and of our Constitution.

It is no accident that we speak of public servants, because with considerable frequency the sovereign citizens go into the polling booth, pull the curtain behind them, and serve as masters. Consent does not mean a contract formed in the past on a particular day. It means continuing consent, respect, affection, and loyalty, given and reaffirmed again and again throughout the decades. I think this is relevant to the serious problems we will face in the future, because we shall need a combination of strength and flexibility if we are to deal with them. A political system which rests upon 210 million pillars is a strong system, relatively safe from earthquakes and storms and tensions within, able to adjust and remain upright. Even in these troubled days, 210 million people around the country are getting on with the nation's business, despite their dismay, hurt, or anger about recent events in our public life.

I am not a member of the gloom and doom chorus. In the middle of the Berlin blockade of 1948, a most dangerous crisis, Secretary of State George C. Marshall was asked how he could remain so calm in the midst of so serious a matter. He replied very tersely, "I've seen it worse." This nation of ours has lived through some dreadful things, and we shall come through these present problems in whatever way is chosen by those who have the constitutional responsibility for making such decisions; the nation will continue to live and will address itself once again to its great national tasks.

Another important notion set forth in the Declaration will require considerable revision, the notion of equality and unalienable rights. In the Declaration it was simply defined as "life, liberty and the pursuit of happiness." We know that the authors had much more in mind, because in 1774 the Congress had addressed a letter to the inhabitants of the Province of Quebec in which many rights were spelled out, and there was, of course, the Virginia Declaration of Rights. These unalienable rights were given more precise and permanent form in the Constitution itself.

The notion of constitutional limits upon the use of raw power is utterly fundamental to the notion of liberty under law. Its steady growth over the centuries makes a very exciting story, one that traces, to use a bit of license, the transformation of the notion that the king can do no wrong into the notion that if it is wrong the king cannot be permitted to do it. There are many elements that went into the process, including some old English judges who, at the risk of their own lives, put their arms around prisoners at the bar and said to the king, "You cannot do this to these men."

But the men of the Continental Congress were men of their times, aware of the limits of the possible, perhaps more concerned about unity and a demand for independence than about giving reality to all of the implied promises of unalienable rights. On this point, after a shameful delay, the American Revolution continues. Giant strides by the courts in the 1950s and by Presidents and the Congress in the 1960s still leave much unfinished business before us. Perhaps not so much now in terms of the law as in terms of what you and I think and do about these matters in our own personal lives.

In the Declaration the notion of unalienable rights was reinforced by what has come to be called the right of revolution. Jefferson mentioned this right, while pointing out that prudence would dictate that we do not change governments for light or transient causes. Perhaps it is not properly a right but a power. Yet it is always there, because at the end of the day you cannot force a free people. They can be led; they can be persuaded; they cannot be forced.

10

Jefferson, with a certain polemical flair, wrote of a "decent respect to the opinions of mankind." Note that "opinions" is in the plural; we might remember that when orators of today invoke a nonexistent "world public opinion." Less than 10 percent of the world's population can now cast a two-thirds vote in the United Nations General Assembly. Only when the General Assembly is virtually unanimous, is it possible to think of a consensus, at least among governments.

Nevertheless, attention to the actual or prospective reactions of governments and peoples in other parts of the world is an important part of policy formulation. This is so whether one thinks of building a durable peace through ever-broadening international cooperation or whether one attempts to analyze power relationships among states. Ideas are also power.

Recalling the main sweep of American foreign policy since World War II, it is not too pretentious to say that it has reflected moderation, responsibility, and generosity far beyond what is acknowledged by those domestic critics who seem to enjoy self-flagellation:

- We demobilized vast conventional military forces almost completely and almost overnight in the wake of World War II.
- We proposed (in the Baruch plan) to turn all fissionable materials over to the United Nations to be used solely for peaceful purposes, with the idea that no nation, including ourselves, would have nuclear weapons.
- We mobilized large resources to bind up the wounds of war and even larger resources to assist developing nations with their urgent struggle for economic and social progress.
- We welcomed fourscore new nations into the world community, sometimes offending old friends and allies in the process.
- We have strongly supported the United Nations and its family of international organizations and the further development and strengthening of international law.
- Where there has been famine or natural disaster, we have been in the forefront of those trying to help.
- And whatever one might now think of the struggles in Korea and Southeast Asia, we sacrificed both men and

treasure to help far-distant peoples to fend off attempts to impose unwanted political systems by force of arms.

There have been mistakes, disappointments, and disillusionment. But, after all, international relations is that part of our public business which we ourselves cannot control. There are about 140 governments on the international scene, no one of which simply salutes when we speak. We would do ourselves deep injury, however, if we let disappointment and discouragement drive us into a new cycle of isolation. There are now major differences between our world and that of the Continental Congress. Our present national problems cannot be solved except through a high degree of international action and cooperation.

I see coming into being a family of man as an organic community—not world government—which will be rooted in harsh necessity rather than a sense of brotherhood. I am profoundly optimistic about the long run, however complex and painful are the problems on our plates at the moment. Perhaps it is an article of faith, but I believe that mankind can be rational at the end of the day, even if in the early morning we can all be pretty ridiculous.

Some of our problems are threatening to outstrip the capacity of the mind of man, but I ask you to recall John F. Kennedy's remark that problems created by man can be solved by man. Whether one believes that or not, is there any choice but to try? It will require imagination, hard work, wisdom, restraint, and sacrifice. As we approach the 200th year of our Republic, we should not be unduly ashamed to say to ourselves that the American people at their best are a very good people. Calling forth our best is not only for political leaders, but for our homes, churches, schools, universities, news media and, most of all, for each one of us sovereign citizens in the impenetrable reflections of his or her inmost thoughts. Self-criticism and what the poet called "divine discontent" have achieved miracles, but self-flagellation can be self-destructive.

In the Continental Congress was a group of men who dared to build upon hope and confidence, not fear and disunity. As we continue with the tasks which face us over the next decades, we shall find other times, other issues, and other gleaming moments when we can and must come together and pledge our lives, our fortunes, and our sacred honor.

DO NOT REMOVE
CARD FROM POCKET